REFORGING EXCALIBUR

CREATING A SUSTAINABLE AND RELEVANT DEFENSE FOR 21ST-CENTURY AMERICA

WILLIAM S. LIND & JOHN EWALD

REFORGING EXCALIBUR

CREATING A SUSTAINABLE AND RELEVANT DEFENSE FOR 21ST-CENTURY AMERICA

ARKTOS
LONDON 2022

ISBN	978-1-914208-87-4 (Paperback)
	978-1-914208-88-1 (Ebook)
EDITING	Constantin von Hoffmeister
COVER & LAYOUT	Tor Westman

⊕ Arktos.com   🅵 fb.com/Arktos   ✈ @arktosmedia   🄾 arktosmedia

WILLIAM S. LIND & JOHN EWALD

REFORGING EXCALIBUR

CREATING A SUSTAINABLE AND RELEVANT DEFENSE FOR 21ST-CENTURY AMERICA

ARKTOS
LONDON 2022

ISBN	978-1-914208-87-4 (Paperback)
	978-1-914208-88-1 (Ebook)
EDITING	Constantin von Hoffmeister
COVER & LAYOUT	Tor Westman

Arktos.com   fb.com/Arktos   @arktosmedia   arktosmedia

Contents

Introduction

THE AMERICAN MILITARY is today the most powerful in the world — for one kind of war. Mostly, it is designed, equipped, and trained for war with other states. This is not surprising, because from the Peace of Westphalia in 1648 until the last few decades, war has been dominated by states. Most people automatically think of war in that context: the army, navy, and air force of one state or an alliance of states fighting the same forces on the other side — army against army, navy against navy, and air force against air force. Some people now refer to this kind of war as "symmetrical" warfare.

Both of America's recent Persian Gulf wars were initially symmetrical wars. The armed forces of the U.S. and its allies swept away the state armed forces of Iraq with ease. But then something the George W. Bush administration did not expect, though the authors of this book certainly did, faced our armed forces in a different kind of war. A variety of armed groups, operating in the vacuum created by the collapse of the Iraqi state, began to fight the American occupiers. This war proved anything but easy for the U.S. armed forces. We were trapped for almost a decade in asymmetrical warfare, at the cost of more than 5,000 American lives and several trillion dollars of expense, which, in the end, resulted in failure. The measure of victory in this kind of war is whether, when you depart, you leave behind a functioning state. We did not, as ISIS's subsequent sweep through Iraq demonstrated.

Today, American troops are still stuck in Iraq, and there appears to be no prospect of a real Iraqi state on the horizon. The same has been the case elsewhere when we have fought asymmetrical wars — wars against enemies who are not states, i.e., in such places as Syria, Somalia, Libya, and Afghanistan. As powerful as America's armed forces are against state enemies who fight as we do, against non-state, asymmetrical, "Fourth-Generation-war" opponents, they lose.

That is one reason for this book. The United States needs armed forces designed for wars of the future, not the past. Another is that current levels of expenditure on the U.S. military are not sustainable. The defense budget itself is about $750 billion annually. The Senate Budget Committee's "National Defense Function," a broader measurement, tops a trillion dollars.

Why is this not sustainable? Because we are running an annual federal budget deficit of about a trillion dollars a year, money we must borrow. (As we write, the 2020 deficit is heading to at least five trillion, thanks to the coronavirus.) This appears sustainable at the moment only because central banks have flooded the world economy with vast excesses of liquidity, which has kept interest rates artificially low. That works for a while, but we have seen time and time again where it leads: to a debt crisis followed by either rising interest rates or rapid inflation or both. When the inevitable debt crisis hits, we will no longer be able to borrow money at rates we can afford.

At the same time, the American people are facing new threats against which our armed forces are largely irrelevant — with an important exception, the National Guard. They include uncontrolled, illegal immigration along our southern border, a more volatile climate, and crumbling infrastructure. These threats face ordinary Americans with far greater dangers than do Moslem guerrillas hiding in the Hindu Kush. Unfortunately, the budget process is trapped in a series of obsolete categories, so these new threats do not get the resources we need to counter them while hundreds of billions of dollars are spent annually providing for wars with other states that are unlikely to happen.

America's defense budget thus faces three demands for radical change: a shift in warfare away from fighting other states to confronting non-state enemies, a requirement to bring the federal budget as a whole into balance, and a growing need for new funding to secure our borders, prepare for climate volatility, and rebuild our infrastructure. This may seem like an insoluble problem. It is not, so long as we realize that most of what we are buying now for national defense is unnecessary. It is the product, not of thoughtful analysis about future needs, but of rote repetition of spending patterns established during the Cold War. The world has changed but the federal government's budget has not.

The rest of this book will show how our defense establishment can make a long-overdue transition from the 20th to the 21st century.

PART I

Where We Are

FROM THE FALL OF Baghdad in the Second Persian Gulf War onwards, the wars America has fought have been not against other states but against non-state entities: Iraqi guerrillas loyal to a wide variety of different causes, al-Qaeda, Somali militias, the Taliban, ISIS, and so on. In every case, we have ended up losing. Logically, this would mean our armed forces are now bending every effort to think through how to fight and win this new kind of war.

But that is not happening. Instead, the Defense Department has decided to pretend war is not changing and go back to preparing for conflicts with other states, principally Russia and China. But we are not going to fight conventional wars with Russia or China because both countries are nuclear powers.

So the hundreds of billions of dollars we spend annually on preparing to fight Russia or China are all wasted, every last dime, while the reforms our armed forces need to win against non-state enemies don't happen. We are like the drunk searching under a streetlight for his car keys. He knows he did not drop them there, but that is where he can see.

To turn this around and begin to re-engage with reality, the first thing we need is a new strategy. Our present strategy is laid out in the federal government's official National Defense Strategy (NDS). That document says the two main threats we face are Russia and China, which is to say the NDS is fiction. So disconnected is it from the world around us that it is not a *national* strategy at all. It is merely a National Defense *Budget* Strategy, crafted to justify current levels and patterns of defense spending.

The new strategy we need starts with the most important fact about our 21st-century world: more and more states face a growing crisis of legitimacy. It is possible that the international state system may collapse sometime before the year 2100. Why is that important? Because if the international state system fails, the world will be plunged into chaos.

That is what specialists in international affairs would call "a big deal." They would be seconded by a 17th-century man who remains important today — Thomas Hobbes. As the Israeli military historian Martin van Creveld points out in his important book *The Rise and Decline of the State*, Thomas Hobbes is the internal theorist of the state as Machiavelli is the theorist of the state's external relations. Hobbes' basic point about the state is a simple one: it arose to bring order. Nothing else, just order. Not liberty, not justice, not prosperity, and most certainly not happiness, just order: safety of persons and property. Order remains the state's main primary purpose today because without order you can't have any of those other good things. So long as anyone stronger or better armed than yourself can walk in, take all you have, rape your wife and daughters, then kill you and your family in whatever ways they find most entertaining, your life is nasty, brutish, and short. That is what state failure brings.

Unfortunately, the foreign policy and defense establishment in Washington (aka "the Blob") does not understand this. It has used the vast capability of the American military against other state armed forces to destroy states. The Blob did it in Iraq (a Republican President), in Libya (a Democratic President), in Syria (both), and in Afghanistan (both, in America's longest war). We continue to do it today with little apparent concern for the people who are left living in chaos. The Blob does not care, when it sets out to destroy a state, that we have had no success in restoring states. It does not care that state failure generates millions of refugees, who, pouring into the Global North, bring the disorder they are fleeing with them. All it cares about is that the annual trillion dollars in the "National Defense Function" continue to flow into the customary troughs.

But that is likely to change. With the election of President Donald Trump, the country discovered that it is possible for anti-establishment candidates to win important elections. President Trump was a transitional figure. He will be followed by anti-establishment candidates from both parties, who will be more serious and better able to translate their new visions of America's future into effective action. When that occurs, they, and our country, will need a new National Defense Strategy, grounded in reality, not in memory or greed.

Understanding where we are does not end with the realization that our National Defense Strategy is obsolete. As we have said, the U.S. armed forces are immensely powerful against enemies who fight as they do. But there are other ways to fight, and against those other ways, the American military is much less capable.

The best way to understand where our armed services are in the sweep of time is through an intellectual framework called "The Four Generations of Modern War," which Mr. Lind developed in the late 1980s.[1] Militarily, the modern era began with the Peace of Westphalia in 1648, which ended the Thirty Years' War. In and after that treaty, states asserted and established a monopoly on war.[2]

Before Westphalia, many different entities fought wars. Religions fought wars; races and tribes fought wars; families, city-states, and business enterprises all fought wars. They used many different means

---

1   See "The Changing Face of War: Into the Fourth Generation" by William S. Lind, Col. Keith Nightengale USA, Capt. John F. Schmitt USMC, Col. Joseph W. Sutton USA and Lt. Col. Gary I. Wilson USMC, *Marine Corps Gazette*, October, 1989.

2   See *The Transformation of War* by Martin van Creveld, (The Free Press, New York, NY 1991).

to fight their wars, not just their own armies and navies. Fighters
ranged from paid mercenaries (now making a comeback) to every boy
or man able to carry a weapon. War was not just Clausewitz's "politics
carried on by other means" but everything from striving to impress
the local girls to a path to eternal salvation (also coming back). In pe-
riods of disorder, such as that between the fall of the Middle Ages and
the rise of the state, wide areas were dominated by wandering bands
of armed men who hired themselves out as soldiers when they could
and otherwise took what they wanted from anyone too weak to resist
them.[3]

States, as they arose over several centuries and extended their writ
around the world, put a stop to all that. We now automatically think
of war as fighting between state armed services, armies against armies,
navies against navies, air forces against air forces. It has been that way
for about 370 years.

Within those 370 years, there have been three "generations" (dia-
lectically qualitative shifts) of war.

- **First Generation war** was fought with line and column tactics. It
lasted from the late 17th century until around the time of the American
Civil War. Its importance for us today is that the First Generation
battlefield was usually a battlefield of order, and the battlefield of order
created a dominant culture of order within state militaries. Most of
the things that define the difference between "military" and "civilian" — saluting, uniforms, careful gradations of rank, etc. — are products of the First Generation and exist to reinforce a military culture
of order. Just as most state militaries are still designed to fight other
state militaries, so they also continue to embody the First Generation
culture of order.

However, starting in the middle of the 19th century, the orderli-
ness of the battlefield began to break down. In the face of mass armies,
nationalism that made soldiers want to fight, and technological

---

3   Ibid.

developments — such as the rifled musket, the breechloader, barbed wire, and machine guns —, the old line-and-column tactics became suicidal. But as the battlefield became more and more disorderly, state militaries remained locked into a culture of order. In effect, they found (and find) themselves with one foot on the dock and one foot on the boat as the two drift ever further apart. This is one reason why state militaries have so much difficulty in Fourth Generation war, where not only is the battlefield disordered, so is the entire society where the conflict is taking place.

- **Second Generation war** was developed by the French Army during and after World War l. It dealt with the increasing disorder of the battlefield by attempting to impose order on it. Second Generation war, also known as firepower/attrition warfare, relied on centrally controlled indirect artillery fire, carefully synchronized with infantry, cavalry, and aviation, to destroy the enemy by killing his soldiers and blowing up his equipment. In effect, the Second Generation attempts to reduce man's most complex activity, war, simply to putting firepower on targets.

Second Generation war preserved the military culture of order. Second Generation armed forces focus inward on orders, rules, processes, and procedures. There is a "school solution" for every problem. Battles are fought methodically, so prescribed methods are required, learned by rote, drive training and education, where the goal is perfection of detail in execution. The Second Generation military culture, like the First, values obedience over initiative (initiative is incompatible with "synchronization") and relies on imposed discipline.

The United States Army and U.S. Marine Corps both learned Second Generation war from the French Army during and after World War l and it largely remains the "American way of war" today. The Marine Corps' formal doctrine is Third Generation war, but it does not follow its doctrine.

- **Third Generation war**, also called maneuver warfare, was developed by the German Army during World War 1. Third Generation war dealt with the disorderly battlefield not by trying to impose order on it but by adapting to disorder and taking advantage of it. Third Generation war relied less on firepower than on speed and tempo. It sought to present the enemy with unexpected and dangerous situations faster than he could cope with them, pulling him apart mentally as well as physically.

The German Army's new tactics were the first non-linear tactics. Instead of trying to hold a line in the defense, the object was to draw the enemy in, then cut him off, putting whole enemy units "in the bag." On the offensive, the German "storm-troop tactics" of 1918 flowed like water around enemy strong points, reaching deep into the enemy's rear while rolling his forward units up from the flanks and rear. These World War 1 infantry tactics, when used by armored and mechanized formations in World War ll, became known as *Blitzkrieg*.

Just as Third Generation war broke with linear tactics, it also broke with the First and Second Generation culture of order. Third Generation militaries focus outward on the situation, the enemy, and the result the situation requires. Leaders at every level are expected to get that result, regardless of orders. Military education is designed to develop military judgment, not teach processes or methods, and most training is force-on-force free play because only free play approximates the disorder of combat. Third Generation military culture values initiative over obedience, tolerating mistakes so long as they do not result from timidity, and it relies on self-discipline rather than imposed discipline, because only self-discipline is compatible with initiative.

When Second and Third Generation war met in combat in the German campaign against France in 1940, the Second Generation French Army was defeated quickly and completely; the campaign was over in six weeks. Both armies had similar technology, and the French actually had more (and better) tanks. Ideas, not weapons, dictated the outcome.

Despite the clear military superiority of Third Generation war over Second, most if not all state militaries today are Second Generation. The reason is cultural: they cannot make the break with the culture of order that the Third Generation requires. Their natural inclination toward the culture of order is reinforced by layers of peacetime bureaucracy; the more resources a military is given, the more bureaucracy it generates. Most state militaries today are not fighting entities at all. They are simply armed bureaucracies, whose main mission is to acquire and justify resources.

- **Fourth Generation war.** Into the orderly garden of Second Generation militaries, Fourth Generation war is hurling itself like a hand grenade. All around the world, state militaries find themselves fighting, not other state militaries, but people waging war for causes and entities that are either smaller or larger than a state. Almost everywhere, state militaries are losing, despite having vast technological superiority and almost infinitely greater resources.

The previous generations were all defined by changes in how war is fought. That is not true of Fourth Generation war, although it yields changes in that, too. As Martin van Creveld has written, what changes in Fourth Generation war (he calls it "non-trinitarian warfare," referring to Clausewitz's trinity of people, government, and army) is who fights and what they fight for. These are greater changes than alterations in how war is fought.

In the Fourth Generation, the state loses the monopoly on war it established after the Treaty of Westphalia. Past is prologue, as once again many different entities fight wars: cartels (which are business enterprises); gangs; races and ethnic groups; causes, such as "animal rights" and environmentalism; religions and ideology — the variety is endless. As was true before the rise of the state, they use many different types of fighters, from child suicide bombers through masses of immigrants. Invasion by immigration is more, not less, dangerous than invasion by a foreign army, because armies eventually go home but immigrants who will not acculturate permanently change the society they invade.

At the core of Fourth Generation war lies a crisis of legitimacy of the state. As states become the preserve of small elites that live very well off the state's ruin, people all around the world are transferring their primary loyalty to things other than the state. Many of those doing so would never fight for the state, but they are willing, even eager, to fight for their new primary loyalty. And so failing states give birth to Fourth Generation war.

The U.S. armed forces have little ability to win Fourth Generation wars because the Second Generation reduces war to putting firepower on targets and doing that brings strategic defeat in the Fourth Generation. You cannot win a contest for legitimacy by killing people and blowing things up. In terms of where war is going, our country now pays about $750 billion a year to fund an obsolete and increasingly useless military. It can fight Fourth Generation wars, as it has in Iraq and Afghanistan, but it cannot win them. We should at least be able to buy defeat for less money.

This picture gets worse. As our obsolescent services prepare for Second Generation wars we are not going to fight, our nation's political leaders have used the control the Constitution gives them over the military to make our armed services guinea pigs in radical social and cultural experiments. These in turn promise to take us from a military that can't win to one that won't fight.

Of these "experiments against reality," to borrow Roger Kimball's phrase, the most damaging is filling the ranks with women, including in combat units. As every previous generation knew, men and women are not interchangeable. Their traditional social roles reflect their inherent differences. Women have important roles in war; the most important is urging their men to fight. But most women are neither physically nor psychologically able to function effectively as soldiers.

In combat, most of them will simply collapse. When a woman platoon leader in the infantry cannot physically perform the mission, what are the men in her platoon supposed to do, carry her?

The greatest damage women's presence inflicts on our military, however, comes not from their incapacity. It is the product of what their presence does to the men around them.

Every study ever done of why men fight has found that the key variable is unit cohesion. Men fight because they do not want to let their friends down. But for a unit to become friends, a "band of brothers," it cannot include women. If it does, instead of cohering, the men see each other as rivals for the women's favors. Have no illusion that it is possible to put young men and young women together in close quarters and not end up with a bordello. I asked the captain of one of the U.S. Navy's amphibious transports, a man I knew, what the ship's fraternization rate was — fraternization meaning women officers having sex with male sailors, something regulations strictly forbid. After being sure no one could hear us — "committing truth" about any of these social experiments is a career-ender — he answered, "100% of course, what do you think? I've had sailors in knife fights over the women officers." At that point, you no longer have a navy.

The problem is exacerbated by a stifling atmosphere of "political correctness," upheld by what are effectively commissars, so-called "equal opportunity officers." If a woman accuses a man of "sexual harassment," which can be anything she thinks it is, including giving her an order she does not like, the man finds himself taken out of his chain of command and thrown into a system where he is presumed guilty until proven innocent. The commissar system he finds himself caught up in is heavily weighted in favor of the woman. The man's career is on the line.

This, in turn, puts the men in our military in an impossible position. They dare not "offend" a woman, so they must be afraid of the women. They cannot ask them to do any task they do not want to do. The woman may be "offended" and make a charge of "sexual harassment" if the man makes advances toward her — in our species, as in most, the male usually takes the initiative in seeking sex — or if he does not do so when she wants him to. What kind of fighting man will stay in a military under these conditions? He will get out and find other ways to fight, which Fourth Generation entities will be happy to offer him. In the face of intense combat, with the real fighters gone or hating what their service does to them, such "militaries" will break and run.

There is icing on that cake: even before panic sets in, the men will drop their unit's mission to protect the women. This is human nature. Any men who know what combat involves will be the first to move to protect and evacuate the women, because they will have at least some idea what happens to women who are captured on a battlefield. In World War ll, the German Wehrmacht included a significant number of women. They were not soldiers, but headquarters assistants. The Germans' memories of what happened to those women who were captured by the Red Army in 1944 when Army Group Center collapsed were so searing that until recently, the German constitution (*Grundgesetz*) forbade all women in the Bundeswehr (there too, feminism triumphed and women now fill the ranks).

A military stuffed with women may suffice for the "hi-tech" fantasy of war that now grips the U.S. military, where "soldiers" and "airmen" sit at consoles stateside and "fly" drones halfway around the world. Women can fight that kind of war. Unfortunately, so far it hasn't worked, and we keep losing. If and when real war with a competent opponent hits our womanized armed forces, they will collapse in a flash.

Filling our armed services with women is the most damaging of the social experiments but it is not the only such folly. Permitting open homosexuals in the military is also problematic. The hypermasculine type are usually tolerable from other troops' perspectives and can be good fighters. But most straight soldiers loathe and despise effeminate gays. If they have to serve near them or, worse, take orders from them, they will become alienated from their service. In combat, effeminate gays are likely to suffer not-so-friendly fire.

The absurd "transgendered" business shows just how far our society has departed from reality. Whether in the military or in society at large, we are talking about a tiny number of mentally ill narcissists. One retired Marine Corps general said, "We [the Marine Corps] must spend millions and millions of dollars to accommodate these people. Do you know how many of them we have? Six."

An essay written many years ago, titled "Killers, Fillers, and Fodder," argued that militaries have three types of people. The killers are few in number but highest in importance, because they are the men who in the chaos of combat will take the initiative and get results. The fillers won't do that on their own, but they will follow the killers. The fodder, the most numerous type, just stand around waiting to be killed. The social experiments — women, gays, and the "transgendered" — drive the killers out. Once they are gone, we will have services that are armed but cannot fight. The price of the experiments against reality will be paid in defeats and in increased American casualties.

In our survey of where we are, we have seen that the U.S. armed forces are focused anew on yesterday's type of war, war with other states; they are saddled with a misoriented strategy; they are not one but two generations of war behind, leaving us to fight Fourth Generation wars with a Second Generation military; and they suffer from a variety of social and cultural experiments against reality, to the point where they begin to suggest a high-budget production of Marat/Sade. To that list, we must add one more assessment: their collective budget far exceeds what is sustainable. This is the most important of their misalignments with reality, because it will compel changes in the other four.

At the same time that the "National Defense Function" in America's federal budget is around a trillion dollars, we are also running annual deficits of about a trillion dollars (again, far more in 2020). Obviously, defense spending is a large share of the "discretionary" federal budget, the portion that is not absorbed by so-called "entitlements" (many of which shouldn't exist). If we are not going to reduce — and eventually eliminate — our deficits, a lot of the reduction must come from defense.

Recently retired Marine General Joseph Dunford, then the Chairman of the Joint Chiefs of Staff, testified to Congress that the greatest threat America faces is its own federal deficits and debt. He was correct. Both political parties have bought into the comforting message that "deficits don't matter." That allows them to fund all their pet projects and interests without raising taxes. So what if the federal government must borrow trillions of dollars a year?

History tells us deficits and debts do matter. Over and over, countries have tried to pay for what they want with endless deficits and debts. The result is always the same: a debt crisis. At a certain point, lenders start to get nervous about their principal being repaid. This is not necessarily a rational calculation, because markets are not rational. They swing, sometimes abruptly, between greed and fear. The swings can be motivated by anything, from excessive exuberance in markets to bad weather in Kansas to a coronavirus. When lenders get nervous, they need to be reassured or they won't lend. The reassurance comes in the form of rising interest rates; rising rates are an attempt to stimulate greed when fear is in control. At some point, rates rise so high governments cannot afford to borrow more. That's what brought about the French Revolution, among other unhappy events.

This time isn't different. All over the world, levels of both private and public debt have been exploding for more than a decade. At some point, events will cause lenders to get nervous and (currently low) interest rates will rise, probably abruptly. At that point, the party's over. We will face a full-scale debt crisis.

A debt crisis is not another garden-variety recession. It brings a depression, one that may be long-lasting. When governments can no longer borrow, they have two choices. They can cut spending not just to but below their income from taxes and use the surplus to start paying off the debts. Or, they can inflate the currency and attempt to repay their debts with worthless money. The second is politically easier than the first, but it leads to hyperinflation, the wiping out of the middle class and complete economic collapse, of the sort we have seen recently in Venezuela.

It is not difficult to see that yielding the Hindu Kush to the Taliban or leaving Europe to defend itself are preferable to a debt crisis, a depression and hyperinflation. If we are to avoid a debt crisis, a reduction in the defense budget — a big one — will have to be a part of our newly prudent course.

This cloud has a silver lining: the reforms we need to strategy, doctrine, and force structure can leave us with more relevant and effective armed forces at a much lower cost.

It is time to move on and see where we need to go and how to get there.

PART II

Where We Need to Go

B ROADLY, we need to go to a new, sustainably affordable defense posture that addresses the real threats Americans face. That begins with a new National Defense Strategy. The new NDS should seek to counter two kinds of threats to Americans: international and internal.

Internationally, the real threats are not Russia, China, or any other state. They are a wide variety of non-state entities that fight Fourth Generation war, including but not limited to Islamic terrorist organizations, such as al-Qaeda and ISIS, Mexican drug cartels, and what is perhaps the most dangerous form of Fourth Generation war: mass movements of would-be immigrants from the Global South to the Global North. Flooding one culture with people from another is much more likely to destroy the former than are random shootings and suicide bombers.

As we said earlier, the Fourth Generation challenge is to the state system itself. The main objective, then, of our National Defense Strategy should be to shore it up. To that end, we need an alliance of all states in defense of the state system. "All states" means precisely that: all states, whether democracies or dictatorships, oligarchies or monarchies. The U.S. would no longer tell other nations how they should govern themselves.

An alliance of all states must begin with an alliance of the three Great Powers in our 21st-century world: the United States, China, and Russia. Why? Because if these three are not allied, instead of uniting all states in defense of the state system we will perpetuate a world of blocs of states in conflict. On the other hand, if the three Great Powers are allied, no country can stay out of the alliance of all states. Any state that tried to oppose the united three Great Powers would be doomed to isolation.

The first collective action of the new alliance would be to prevent all conflicts between states. This can begin as soon as the three Great Powers are allied. The new Triple Alliance would start by attempting to mediate existing state conflicts: North and South Korea, India and Pakistan, Israel and Iran, and so on. Mediation by the Triple Alliance would be the iron hand in the velvet glove: any state which refused to settle its conflict with another state would soon face more pressure, especially economic pressure, than it could bear.

For the United States, the new Triple Alliance and, as soon as it can be formed, the alliance of all states would mean our military would no longer be structured, trained, and equipped for fighting other states. As we have seen in Iraq, Libya, and Afghanistan, wars with other states lead to the destruction of those states and a new petri dish of Fourth Generation war, which will be the opposite of our purpose. We would retain a residual, mostly naval force intended to combat other state forces as an insurance policy. But thanks to our geography, we face no land threats from another state, either now or in prospect. We would also retain the most effective counter to any serious threat from another state, our strategic nuclear deterrent.

History has seen a number of attempts to end war between states, such as the Kellogg-Briand Pact, all of which have failed. Why is this different? Because the only way to keep states from fighting each other is to unite them against a threat to all of them. That, Fourth Generation war now does. The United States, China, and Russia all have faced and face today threats from Fourth Generation entities

on their own soil, including drug cartels' operations across the U.S.–
Mexico border, Islamic separatism in China's western provinces, and
rebellions in some of the Russian Federation's southern republics. Just
as it took the Persians to unite the Greek city-states, so the danger
Fourth Generation war presents to all states can unite them now.

What sort of military capabilities does the new Triple Alliance
(which will remain the main decision-maker in the alliance of all
states) require to uphold failing states around the world? And which
of those capabilities is America best suited to provide? Here is where
Fourth Generation war poses a difficult challenge.

Trying to uphold and restore not just the control but the legitimacy of a failing state from outside is problematic. Such attempts face
an inherent contradiction, in that foreign support for one side or
another (in this case, always the existing state) in an internal conflict
undermines the legitimacy of whoever is receiving the support. This
is a subset of an inherent problem in Fourth Generation war: what
works on the physical and tactical levels often leads to defeat on the
moral and strategic levels.

As the U.S. found in Afghanistan and Russia may discover in
Syria, foreign forces that fight to extend the state's physical control
of territory simultaneously undermine that state's legitimacy. While
the enemy or the conflict itself may be suppressed, it is likely soon to
break out again when the foreign forces leave.

In Fourth Generation war, victory means leaving a real, self-sus-
taining state, one that has and can maintain a monopoly of violence
on its territory and that can gradually accrue legitimacy. A facade of
a state that crumbles as soon as the next Fourth Generation threat
arises, such as the Iraqi state America left behind that collapsed in
the face of ISIS or the Communist state the Soviets left behind in
Afghanistan (and probably the one we will leave there as well) is not
victory. It is merely fig leaves covering the shame of defeat.[1]

---

1   See *Fourth Generation Warfare Handbook* by William S. Lind and Lt. Col.
    Gregory A. Thiele, USMC (Castalia House, Kouvola, Finland, 2015).

The members of the Triple Alliance, and other states as they join the alliance of all states, will have to determine what capabilities each can bring to the common pot, in terms of creating a combined capability not only to fight but to win Fourth Generation conflicts on other countries' soil. For the U.S., those may be mostly technological, especially covert surveillance capabilities.

Perhaps the most important factor in efforts to prop up or restore collapsing states is what external actors must not attempt to do, namely remake the state in question in their own image. This is a besetting sin of the American foreign policy establishment, and it guarantees failure. Forcing Jacobin definitions of "human rights," such as feminism and "gay rights," on other countries and cultures assures our efforts will delegitimize the state we are attempting to support. For a state to be legitimate, it must reflect the culture and history of its own people. External efforts, such as those U.S. forces may be part of, must focus on restoring order — safety of persons and property — and not remaking the society in question. As the great conservative man of letters Russell Kirk said, there is no surer way of making a man your enemy than by telling him you are going to remake him in your image for his own good.

The Triple Alliance, and the larger alliance of all states, will have to evolve their military capabilities so as to provide suitable forces for state preservation. We cannot foresee exactly how that evolution will proceed. In general, it is safe to say that military capabilities developed to fight other states are likely to prove irrelevant or counter-productive to the alliance's task.

Thus we see in broad terms where we need to go for dealing with overseas threats in a world of failing states and rising Fourth Generation war. But what about here at home? After all, the first and most important purpose of national defense is to protect Americans in their own country, states, and communities.

Serving this purpose effectively requires us to broaden our definition of national defense. What actually most endangers American citizens on their own soil? The first answer is, Fourth Generation war fought within America itself.

As many a big-city police department will tell you, that is already happening. The largest source of such warfare here at home is massive communities of immigrants, legal and illegal, who have not been Americanized, i.e., acculturated into long-standing American ways of living and behaving. American culture is, in terms of its origins and characteristics, and moving from general to specific, Christian, white, Northern European and Anglo-Saxon. That culture has been and remains the basis for America's success, its order, its liberties and its prosperity. If traditional American culture is overwhelmed by a sea of immigrants from other cultures — in our case, largely the mestizo culture of Mexico and Central America — we will become like the places those people are fleeing. America, too, will be a disordered, unsafe, and increasingly poor Third World country.

America successfully absorbed earlier waves of immigrants because the entire American establishment was united on a policy of Americanization. Today, that same establishment promotes an ideal of "multiculturalism," telling immigrants they should not adopt American culture. Nothing is more conducive to generating widespread Fourth Generation war on American soil. Put bluntly, multicultural countries break up in bloody civil wars. The cultural Marxists who gave birth to "multiculturalism" welcome that: it helps them attain their objectives of destroying Western culture, the Christian religion and the white race. To any American who loves his country and wants to see it endure, "multiculturalism" should be poison.

Enclaves of immigrants who have not (and in the case of Moslems will not) acculturate have already become a base for Fourth Generation war here at home. We see that most dramatically in increased crime rates and the rise of violent, ethnically based gangs. Hyper-violent Mexican cartels are now operating in parts of the United States, and they seek to undermine our state just as they have the Mexican state, which is now weaker on its own soil than the three main cartels.

But not all gangs are foreign in origin. Gangs and cartels, which are illegal business enterprises that fight, are also born right here in the U.S.A. Most are racially based, some black, some white. If you want to see what an America beset by Fourth Generation war looks like, look in our prisons, where everything is run by ethnically based gangs and no one has any security outside a gang.

It doesn't stop there. Adherents to a wide variety of "causes" and ideologies, from "animal rights" and "Deep Green environmentalism" to both white and black nationalists who want racially pure states on American soil, are also practicing Fourth Generation war when they initiate violence. An environmentalist who buries a saw blade in a tree, hoping to kill a logger, is committing an act of war, not just a crime. So is a black man who shoots a white cop just sitting in his cruiser in a black part of town. He is attacking the officer as a symbol of the state and what the state exists to guarantee: order.

The most important challenge, by far, that Fourth Generation war poses is not the threat it presents to other states but the danger it represents to us here at home. The worst thing that can happen to us is widespread Fourth Generation war on American soil. Preventing that should be the top national security goal of both political parties and of everyone in Washington. Unfortunately, at present, no one in Washington seems even to recognize the danger. As Martin van Creveld, the Israeli historian whose book *The Transformation of War* is foundational to Fourth Generation war theory, said to Mr. Lind in his office on Capitol Hill, "Everyone can see it except the people in the capital cities."

Redefining national security to make it relevant to the 21st century, not the 20th, does not stop here. Again we must pose the question: what actually threatens Americans in their homes and communities? High on the list comes globalism, unimpeded flows of people, things and money around the world.

From that perspective, the coronavirus has served as a wake-up call. It may or may not have been natural in origin. But either way, it dramatically illustrated one of the perils of globalism: pandemics.

Science has by no means conquered epidemic diseases. Quite the contrary: the hideous technology of genetic engineering guarantees new plagues, both as a result of accidents and created as weapons of mass destruction. While states, fearing blowback, will be reluctant to employ such weapons, Fourth Generation entities may not be. If ISIS launched a plague that killed 100,000,000 Moslems, it would just shrug and say, "They are all martyrs."

Globalism has already done great damage to America by shifting millions of good jobs, jobs that paid enough to support a family, to other countries. Our blue-collar middle class, which was the backbone of manufacturing cities, such as Cleveland, has almost vanished. Our industrial economy offered millions of intermediate-skill, high-paying jobs, jobs where people worked with their hands and made good money. Now we have a few high-skill, high-paying jobs where people work with their minds and millions of low-skill, low-wage jobs that pay too little to support a middle-class standard of living. America's greatest achievement was creating a country where almost everyone was part of the middle class. Globalism killed that America.

Now, globalism threatens to kill everybody. A world where people, things, and money travel endlessly everywhere cannot stop a plague. If it appears in one country, as the coronavirus did, it is fated to appear in every country. Luckily, the coronavirus had a low death rate, less than 1%. Genetically engineered plagues will be far more dangerous. They could easily return us to the days of the Black Death, the plague, where in a typical six-weeks visitation one-third to two-thirds of the population died. In some places, everyone fell dead, and the village or town remains uninhabited today.

Surviving in a world of genetic engineering will mean the end of globalism. It may mean that security becomes not just national but local. During the coronavirus epidemic, we saw some states close their

borders to people from other states. States and localities may have
to be able to meet their own basic needs in everything, starting with
food. The implications of that for the future of the nation-state are all
too clear. Having moved from feudalism to the state to globalism, we
may abandon first globalism and then the state for feudalism.

Since our goal is to preserve the nation-state, we must block that
path. Doing so means the state must be able to protect us effectively
from pandemic diseases, regardless of their source. That, in turn, requires an ability to shut a country down tight on very short notice.
The entry of both people and things must be completely blocked.
Since globalism depends on free global movement of both people and
things, the United States must abandon globalism. We need not to go
full autarky, but we should be able to get by on what we grow, make or
mine here if we have to. Since international flows of money respond
strongly, and often destructively, to epidemics, we must no longer
depend on those either. All of this may sound radical and threatening,
but it would merely return the United States to the way things were in
the 1950s. As those of us who were alive then can tell you, the 1950s
were good years.

The necessity of taking full control of our borders to stop plagues
will enable us to stop illegal immigrants as well. As climate volatility,
economic collapse, state failure and Fourth Generation war ravage the
Global South, millions of people there will try to move to the Global
North. We already see this happening around the world.

Put bluntly, we have to stop them. Doing so is likely to require
deadly force and plenty of it. From the state's perspective, it is preferable if the deadly force is passive: minefields, automatic machine
guns, high-voltage electric fences and the like. By using mostly passive
defenses, states can shift the moral calculus. Soldiers shooting down
mothers with children looks bad, though at times it will be necessary.
But if those mothers with children wander into deadly border zones
despite plenty of warnings, people look upon the situation differently.

Instead of the state appearing callous, the would-be immigrants appear stupid.

As Colonel John Boyd argued, the moral level of war is the highest and most powerful. To the degree the situation permits, states should try to shape the physical level of Fourth Generation conflict in ways that also win at the mental and moral levels.

Our country will have to shape legal immigration as well so that it strengthens, not weakens, the state. That will mean taking immigrants from places whose culture is compatible with our own. Where and when we can cream off another country's upper class, who will arrive with both money and skills, that will usually be beneficial to us, even when those people come from different cultures. In general, we should only accept immigrants who will not be a burden on the people already here.

Calling a would-be immigrant a "refugee" should not mean letting him in. They will all call themselves that. True refugees come on an individual basis, single individuals fleeing political persecution aimed specifically at them. They stay only until the situation in their home country improves to where they can safely go home.

Some of the things Americans are threatened by and need to be defended from by the state are not warfare at all. But they have a claim on the Defense Department's vast budget, because almost all of that is spent "defending" us from Russia and China, which are not threats. "National defense" should mean exactly that: defending American citizens against whatever is a threat to their lives, homes and families.

As we have already seen from a stream of worsening storms, the climate is becoming more volatile. That should not surprise us. Since the "Little Ice Age" of the 14th and 15th centuries, we have had the good fortune to live in a period of unusual climate stability. It was bound to end.

The degree to which climate volatility is man-made is in dispute. Nature remains far more powerful than man. Also uncertain is the direction in which the climate will ultimately head: warmer or colder.

All projections are linear, but neither climate nor history move in linear fashion. On the whole, a colder climate would create more problems for Americans than a warmer climate. We can protect Miami
from rising sea levels, but what would Cleveland do if it were under
a mile of ice?

Increasingly volatile weather does seem likely in the near future.
Most of our active-duty military is irrelevant to helping people when
it happens. One of our services, the National Guard (both Army and
Air Guard), is highly relevant. When tornadoes, hurricanes, floods
and fires hit, we quickly turn to the National Guard for rescue and
assistance. So do our police and fire departments. As we will see in
our next section, we need to put more resources into the National
Guard, and we need to strengthen it in other ways as well. In a world
of Fourth Generation war, our most important and valuable armed
service is the National Guard.

For the most part, what we need to do to make America more
resilient in the face of increasingly volatile weather falls beyond the
purview of the military. It includes erecting new defenses against
coastal and riverine flooding, wind-proofing buildings, managing
forests more wisely and offering larger and more comprehensive
packages of assistance to people who suffer losses to violent weather.
Because climate volatility is a greater threat to Americans than Russia
or China, real national defense means shifting resources away from
the Pentagon toward agencies, state as well as federal, that protect us
from violent weather and help us recover after we get hit by it.

Nor does redefining national defense stop there. In the 1950s,
when President Eisenhower wanted to build the Interstate Highway
System, he presented it to Congress as necessary for national defense.
We do not need more roads, but we urgently need to keep the roads
and bridges we have, along with our water supply and sewage systems
(many of which include miles of 19th-century pipes) and the rest of
our infrastructure, in good condition. Much of it is not, reflecting decades of deferred maintenance due to inadequate funding. Collapsing

bridges, crumbling highways, unsafe drinking water and poor sewage treatment that re-opens the door to diseases, such as typhoid fever, are greater threats to Americans than are Russia and China. The real should take precedence over the hypothetical and improbable.

In sum, where we need to go, in terms of the real threats we face, is to a much smaller active-duty military establishment, one oriented toward non-state threats. We also need to re-balance our resources away from purely military threats and toward dealing with a broader menu of threats to ordinary people in their lives at home and at work. All this demands a clean-sheet-of-paper approach to the federal budget, instead of robotically re-funding defense budget lines that trace to the Cold War or even before.

But something else also requires us to re-think our $750-billion defense budget: we can't afford it.

That much money — one trillion dollars annually for the "National Defense Function" — is not sustainable, not in the face of trillion-dollar-plus annual federal deficits (and trillions more in 2020). The only federal budget that is sustainable over the long run is a balanced budget. If we have a balanced budget, we can meet extraordinary needs, such as those created by the coronavirus, without risking a debt crisis, a liquidity freeze or a run on the dollar. If we instead continue to pile up debt, all the latter are only a matter of time.

What defense budget size is sustainable? A reasonable target is $100 billion per year. The next section of this book will show how we can restructure our military to attain that level or something close to it. Remember, the vast bulk of the current budget goes for forces that are useful only in wars against other states. That kind of war is exiting history stage left as Fourth Generation war enters stage right. As that happens, a military designed and equipped for state vs. state warfare becomes a military museum. De-funding a museum should not trouble us unduly.

Reshaping our armed forces to support a National Defense Strategy relevant to the 21st century and affordable over the long haul defines most of where we need to go. But there remains one vital part, one that is often overlooked because it is not directly a spending issue: military reform.

What is military reform? It is changing not what we do but how we operate. The military reform movement of the 1980s raised a number of issues that, for the most part, the Defense Department has never addressed. Yet these issues are central not only to ensuring we get our money's worth when we buy military equipment but to the bottom line of any military: when we fight wars, do we win or lose? Since World War II, the answer has mostly been the latter.

The most important reform if we want to improve our won:lost ratio is moving our armed services from the Second Generation of modern war to the Third, while attempting to prepare for the Fourth. This is a challenging task, because it requires deep changes in institutional culture.

First and Second Generation armed forces share the culture of order. That culture's defining feature is inward focus. Second Generation militaries like ours focus inward on rules, processes, formulae, and orders. There is a process for everything, and what is most important is following the process, not the result. Military education and training are designed to teach processes and inculcate inward focus. Inward focus yields the other defining cultural traits of the Second Generation: centralization of decision-making, preferring obedience to initiative, and depending on imposed discipline rather than self-discipline. In a First or Second Generation military, the worst thing anyone can do is disobey an order.

Third and Fourth Generation militaries have sharply different cultures. These military cultures focus outward on the situation, the enemy, and the result the situation requires. Leaders at every level are required to get that result regardless of orders, rules, processes, etc. Attempting to justify failure by saying "I was just following orders" gets a commander relieved.

Orders, in turn, tell subordinates the final result the commander at least two levels up is trying to attain, his "commander's intent." They offer general guidance in how that might be best accomplished, but subordinates are free to disregard the "how" if they need to in order to get the desired result. Results justify all actions, but a failure to act means immediate relief.

The remainder of Third Generation culture supports outward focus. Initiative is preferred over obedience (in the Prussian Army in the 19th century, it was routine in war games to give junior officers problems that could only be solved by disobeying orders). Decision-making is highly decentralized; as General Mike Myatt, who commanded the First Marine Division in the First Gulf War, puts it, "Maneuver warfare [Third Generation war] is not centralized decision-making and decentralized execution; it is centralized vision and decentralized decision-making." Discipline is primarily self-discipline, because imposed discipline and initiative are in tension with each other. Action in a Third Generation military is much faster than in the Second, because the former are in effect wired in parallel, the latter in series.

The great culture break occurs between the Second and Third Generations; the outward focused culture of the Third carries over into the Fourth. At present, the main task facing the U.S. military in Fourth Generation war is intellectual: figuring out how to fight it.[2]

Shifting our armed services' culture from the Second to the Third Generation means changing everything else, starting with the personnel system. Instead of moving people constantly as individuals, the personnel system must keep units' personnel stable for at least two to three years. At that point, whole units go into the reserve as units, and a new active-duty unit is built from the ground up. Commanders should have their units for at least three to five years, instead of twelve to eighteen months. Personnel stability is necessary for unit cohesion,

---

2   Ibid.

which is the basis of why men fight (or don't), and it also makes possible implicit communication, which is faster and more reliable than explicit communication.[3] Maneuver warfare is based on operating at a higher tempo than the enemy, which is only possible when people are used to working with each other.

Education and training must also be reformed. Instead of teaching what to do, education should teach how to think militarily, how to look at a military situation and see what to do. Most training should be force-on-force free play, where each side is allowed to do whatever it wants in order to win. Currently, most training is scripted, which is appropriate for an opera company but has little to do with war.

For a service to adopt Third Generation doctrine, as the United States Marine Corps did in the early 1990s, but not make these reforms to its personnel system, education and training (which the Marines did not make), there is little payoff. Marines still fight Second Generation war the same way the U.S. Army does. The excellent maneuverist field manuals the Marine Corps issued in the early '90s will be little more than historical footnotes unless the Marine Corps' institutional culture changes. The same is true for our other services: militaries with Second Generation culture cannot win Third or Fourth Generation wars.

Reforms in the way we design, test, and purchase military equipment are also highly important. Without them, we will spend a great deal but receive little in return, as is now the case. It is absurd for one bomber to cost more than a billion dollars (the B-2), or an aircraft carrier $15 billion (a cargo ship can be modified into a perfectly adequate carrier for a fraction of that price). No longer should our services design their equipment to be unique, any more than you would design the car you want, then ask Ford to build it. Most systems should be bought from what is available on the open market, pitting candidates against each other in real fly-offs and shoot-offs, then

---

3   See Col. John Boyd's briefing on Command and Control (unpublished).

buying the winners. When we did the latter, briefly, in the 1980s, we got combat aircraft that performed better and cost less than their predecessors (the F-16 and the A-10), something that has not happened since (we have bought almost 1,000 F-35s before their testing was even complete; a poor fighter, the F-35 is our first trillion-dollar weapon program). Putting it simply, where we need to go in R&D, testing and procurement is from the Soviet economy to a free market economy. Right now the Pentagon runs the world's largest planned economy. Should it surprise us that everything costs too much and does not work very well?

None of these reforms will give us a winning military without one more: ending the use of our armed services as guinea pigs in social "experiments against reality" and undoing the damage such nonsense has already done. First and foremost, that means getting the women out of all our services with one exception: the National Guard.

The overriding purpose of the Army, the Navy, the Air Force and the Marine Corps is to fight. Nothing undermines their ability to do that more than the presence of women, for reasons we have already discussed. They can retain a few women if they want to, in non-deployable clerical and medical roles. But they have no need to do so. They will have no trouble meeting their recruiting goals with men, because their personnel numbers will drop sharply as we reshape them for Fourth Generation war. Along with getting rid of the women we must do the same with effeminate homosexuals or other gays whose behavior undermines fighting spirit. "Don't ask, don't tell" should again become the rule for the gays who join the military.

Why should the National Guard be an exception? Because fighting is only part of the Guard's mission and often it is not the most important part. In humanitarian operations on American soil, the National Guard is not likely to face violent resistance. It is normally welcomed by Americans it is trying to help. Many of those will be women and children, and female National Guardsmen can often comfort them better than men as they face traumatic losses. The Guard will face some combat missions on American soil, on our southern border and probably within our cities. The units it intends to use for those missions should be male-only. But in providing disaster relief, the Guard benefits from having some women in its ranks.

Thus we see where we need to go, our desired end-state and overarching "commander's intent." We want to end up with an American military that can not only fight but win Fourth Generation conflicts of every sort, at home and abroad (with the former far more important), at a budget level that is sustainable over the long haul. As should be clear by now, that is a call for massive change from the military we have. So, how do we get from where we are to where we need to go? That is the subject of the next section of this book.

PART III

How to Get There

A T THE OUTSET, we need to make one thing clear: neither of the authors of this book is a budgeteer. We cannot put exact prices on what our armed services and their equipment will cost after we make the necessary reforms. Our goal of a $100-billion annual defense budget is aspirational. We may not be able to get it down that low. On the other hand, once the inevitable world-wide debt crisis hits, the country may not be able to afford even that much. In the long run, affordability, not desired force structure, will determine the budget level, and force structure will have to be shaped to match. We have chosen a goal of $100 billion because we think it is a useful approximation of what in future will be both sufficient and attainable.

While $100 billion will seem a drastic reduction to the interests that feed richly off our current $750-billion defense budget, it will still leave us with the world's most expensive military. The Pentagon will say China is spending more, but they estimate Chinese costs for military manpower at what we would pay for the same levels of personnel. Of course, the Chinese don't pay that.

To develop a sound understanding of what we need to spend on defense, we must halt the long-standing practice of measuring our defense capability by inputs: more spending equals more capability. You cannot buy victory like chopped liver, by the pound. In war, only outputs count, not inputs. France's Maginot Line cost far more than the few Panzer divisions Germany possessed in 1940, but the German Panzers went around the Maginot Line and rendered all those gold francs a useless waste of money. If we graphed our defense spending against the budgets of al-Qaeda or the Taliban, theirs would not even be visible. But we have yet to defeat either of them, and the Taliban have a right to claim victory as we try to get out of Afghanistan with at least a few tail feathers intact.

The following means to reach our goals may not total exactly what we want on the adding machine. But they represent reforms that will save hundreds of billions of dollars each year and give us armed services appropriate for the wars of the 21st century instead of the 20th. We happily leave the number-crunching to the Senate and House Budget Committees. They actually seem to enjoy it.

Department of Defense (DOD)-level Reforms:

Some of the biggest money-saving reforms apply across all services. They include:

- Greatly reducing forces useful only for wars with other states. We will look at this in detail for each service, but it applies to all with the exception of our strategic nuclear forces and, in part, the Navy.

- Firing virtually all contractors except those who actually build military equipment (equipment that henceforth will be maintained by military personnel, not contractors). Our troops will eat no more steak and lobster dinners courtesy of contractors; they will again run their own mess halls. If equipment is too complex to be maintained by our servicemen, it is too complex for war and we won't buy it. Nothing has damaged our armed services more than contracting out their thinking to retired senior officers, people who created or perpetuated the problems we now hire them to solve. We have many bright junior officers and staff NCOs; they should do our military's thinking in the future, because their experience is in Fourth Generation war. Giving 90% or more of the vast herd of contractors the heave-ho will immediately free up tens if not hundreds of billions of dollars. It will also help re-militarize services that have largely become armed bureaucracies.

- Similarly, we will greatly reduce the horde of civil servants now employed by the Defense Department. Like most of the contractors, they generate bureaucracy, cost us a great deal of money and bring us not one inch closer to victory in war. Most of the work they do is writing memos to each other. If their jobs go undone, no one will notice.

Again, these reforms should apply across all services. They will simultaneously save money and improve our military performance. Next, we will look at each of the DOD's components, where we will quickly see ways to reduce spending without hurting our military capabilities. In fact, many of the needed reforms will help us win.

Strategic Nuclear Forces

In terms of bang for the buck, our strategic nuclear forces are bargains. They don't cost all that much except when major capabilities must be modernized, which is seldom, while they buy us a great deal. Obviously, the first thing they give us is deterrence against a nuclear attack from any other state. But they buy more than that: they make conventional war against other nuclear powers impossible, absent a truly moronic blunder by politicians.

That is why the current National Defense Strategy, which sees conventional wars with China or Russia as the main threat, is a work of fiction. Throughout the whole Cold War, both the U.S. and the Soviet Union were careful not to engage each other's conventional forces directly. When engagements did happen, which was seldom, both sides usually denied they had occurred. The reason is obvious: in an open clash, whoever is losing conventionally comes under enormous domestic political pressure to redeem their defeat by going nuclear. Nuclear war is so dangerous that neither we nor the Soviets wanted to set a single foot on the escalation ladder. The same reasoning applies to the absurd notion of conventional wars with China or Russia now.

A recent DOD war game proved the point. The scenario was the U.S. vs. China in a conventional war, a war that started with a conflict over some strategically meaningless islands in the South China Sea. After the U.S. had taken 150,000 casualties, our commanders were requesting permission to employ nuclear weapons. Their Chinese counterparts were probably doing the same (in a war at sea, China would gain an asymmetric advantage by going nuclear from the outset as the Soviets planned to do, since our navy is based on surface ships and theirs on submarines). If a real war that followed this scenario were to take place, we would end up trading San Diego and Seattle for a few sand spits.

Conversely, were all nuclear weapons to be abolished, the world would again see vast conventional wars like World War II.[1] A de-industrialized and debt-burdened United States would not be the top power in such a world.

The fact is that nuclear weapons in the hands of states are almost always stabilizing. If two hostile states both possess nuclear weapons, neither can risk going to war, even if one is much stronger in conventional forces. We see that in the ongoing hostile relationship between India and Pakistan. India is much stronger in conventional forces, but dares not risk a war because Pakistan has nuclear weapons. But nuclear weapons can be stabilizing even if only one power has them, assuming it acts prudently. The fact that Israel has a sizable nuclear arsenal has put an end to threats from neighboring Arab states and forced a *modus vivendi* on them. They know that if they again attacked Israel and were winning conventionally, Israel would go nuclear. Conventional

---

1   Conversation between Martin van Creveld and William S. Lind.

attacks on Israel such as those we saw in 1948, 1967 and 1973 are now pointless; they cannot result in an Arab victory. In response, several long-hostile Arab countries are now *de facto* Israeli allies, because nothing else makes strategic sense.

The normal year-to-year maintenance of our strategic nuclear forces costs little. Major modernization programs can be costly, and both the Navy and the Air Force are saying they need one, the Navy for its strategic missile submarines and the Air Force both for its land-based ICBMs and for its bomber force. The bomber should be a non-starter. As we will see in our look at the Air Force, we need bombers, but only for Fourth Generation war, which means they can be simple, inexpensive aircraft. Both our ICBMs and our strategic missile submarines will need replacement at some point. Whether that point is now or whether both can be given Service Life Extension Programs at much lower cost is an open question.

Even if such replacement programs do prove necessary for both the Navy and the Air Force, we can substantially reduce their projected cost by going to a posture of minimum deterrence. What that means is that instead of being able to fire thousands of nuclear warheads, we would have only a few hundred or perhaps only dozens. Given their power, it does not take many nuclear weapons to provide effective deterrence. China has done exactly this; its long-range nuclear delivery systems that can hit the United States number fewer than one hundred. They know that is sufficient, and they have no desire to bankrupt themselves building thousands more.

Not only can we negotiate a treaty with Russia to limit how many strategic nuclear weapons each country can possess or deliver, we have such a treaty. It is expiring, and it is in the interest of both countries to renew it. Russia has indicated it favors doing so, but the U.S. is reluctant unless China also signs on. But Chinese participation is not necessary so long as China maintains its minimum deterrence posture, which it shows no signs of abandoning. A treaty between the U.S. and Russia can easily include an escape clause in case a third party does threaten to build a massive arsenal, not that it would gain much from doing so.

There remains one other purpose for nuclear weapons: employing them against non-nuclear adversaries. Doing so against other states would carry the large disadvantage of sparking an almost universal nuclear arms race. Every state that saw itself facing even a potential threat from a nuclear-armed state would strain every nerve to build its own nuclear weapons and delivery systems or buy them from any nuclear power ready to sell. Unless we faced a large and imminent threat from another country that appeared to act irrationally, to the point of wanting to commit suicide, nuclear attacks on our part on non-nuclear states will not be worth the de-stabilization they would inflict on the whole state system, whose stability and strength should be our top strategic goal.

There is, however, a situation in Fourth Generation war where we might choose to employ nuclear weapons, and that is following an attack like 9/11 from a non-state entity, an attack that inflicts major bodily harm on the U.S. here at home. To such an attack, our response should be icy cold, lightning fast and utterly annihilating. Our intent should be to inflict vastly disproportionate damage in a very short amount of time, not only on the entity that struck us, which on 9/11 was al-Qaeda, but on the area hosting that organization, which will usually be a failed or failing state. If the state hosting the group that attacked us is a real state, then it should be hit as a matter of course, because it had to have approved the operation.

As we will see when we discuss the Air Force and the Marine Corps, we want to be able to launch an annihilating attack without using nuclear weapons. But if they offer the only means to respond both immediately and with complete devastation, we should employ them.

To defend ourselves effectively in a world of Fourth Generation war, when entities that attack us on our own soil do so powerfully (which may mean they have already used weapons of mass destruction, either a nuclear weapon or something genetically engineered that creates a plague), our response must be Roman. If someone rebelled against Rome, Rome did whatever it took to destroy their city, kill their men and sell their women and children into slavery. They even cut the dogs in half. Like Rome, we must make a desert and call it peace.

The National Guard

Most books that look at our armed services consider the National Guard last, as an also-ran that probably does not have much relevance. Here, we start with the Guard because in a world of Fourth Generation war, it becomes our most important armed service. Instead of the Army and Air Guard existing to support the regular forces, the regular forces' most important mission becomes supporting the National Guard.

We have already discussed why this is the case: the Guard, both its Army and Air components, has as its top priority mission helping Americans on American soil. Whether our own people need assistance and protection because of natural disasters or because a Fourth Generation entity has struck effectively on American soil, as on 9/11, the National Guard is what governors, mayors, and ordinary people turn to. Unlike the active-duty services, the Guard is comfortable working with other federal and state agencies even if it is not in charge. The Guard pulls people from their flooded houses, helps fight massive forest fires, provides medical care in epidemics and keeps order so both people and their property are secured. In terms of actually defending Americans, these missions are more important than hunting "terrorists" half a world away — many of whom want to do us harm because we have meddled in their backyards.

But there is more to the National Guard's importance in Fourth Generation war than the services it provides. As we said at the beginning, Fourth Generation war is above all a contest for legitimacy. More than a few Americans are uncertain about the legitimacy of the

federal government and its enforcers, including federal police forces
and even the active-duty military, at least when it is employed domes-
tically. But the National Guard is not a federal force. It is responsible
to the states, not Washington. And the people in it are local people,
our own friends and neighbors. No armed element on American
soil has legitimacy that matches the National Guard's. No one fears
Guardsmen, or sees them as threats. Their helicopters are not painted
black.

In turn, helping their neighbors is what leads people to join the
Guard. When we send Guardsmen to places like the Balkans and
Afghanistan, we are misusing them. That is not why they enlisted. A
friend of one of the authors flies helicopters for the National Guard.
His unit was in Kosovo when their home state, Pennsylvania, was hit
with massive flooding. They were asking each other, why the hell are
we here when our people at home need us? It was a legitimate question, and the answer was because they were being mis-employed by
the active-duty military.

Reversing the previous relationship between the National Guard
and the regular forces — so the latter's prime mission is supporting
the former — will bring many changes. For example, Guardsmen's
uniforms should say "National Guard," not "Army" or "Air Force."
But there is one change that is more important than all the others.
The Army and Air National Guards should have their own budgets,
completely separate from the budgets of the active duty services. The
Guard is, after all, a bargain. It gives us 450,000 soldiers and airmen
for about $25 billion a year.

Money is power. At present, the active-duty Army and Air Force
determine what money Guard units get. That means the Guard must
dance to their tune, the tune of war overseas against other states.
Those days are over, and so should be the regular forces' control over
the Guard's budget. In fact, we should probably remove the National
Guard's budget from the Defense Department altogether. The Guard
Bureau in Washington, D.C., should take the Guard's budget request

to Congress every year, without having to go through the DOD, where the active-duty military retain overwhelming influence because they cost much more than the Guard. Senators and congressmen represent their states, and the National Guard's units are state, not federal, armed forces. Members of Congress can talk to their own state's adjutant generals, who command each state's Guard, about what they most need. The less influence the regular forces can exert over the Guard, the better. After all, the National Guard represents America's long militia tradition. Our nation's founders were rightly suspicious of large standing armies that answer only to the national government. Between the two, the Guard wins the legitimacy contest hands down.

The Guard will also need some internal restructuring to suit it better to Fourth Generation war on American soil. Obviously, it cannot employ the "American way of war," which means massive use of firepower, in America. We don't want to destroy American cities in order to "save" them, as we did in Iraq to Fallujah and Mosul. Artillery, tanks, and other major supporting arms will be of little use to the Guard with its new focus. Light infantry that employs tactics not dependent on massive firepower, engineer units, field hospitals, communications units that can operate when civilian networks are down, truck units that can deliver food and water, rescue helicopters and ambulance aircraft: these will be the units state governors need. Older equipment is often better, because it still works if electronics have been fried, something massive solar flares or electro-magnetic pulse (EMP) weapons can do.

For the most part, even when dealing with Fourth Generation war, the Guard, like police, will be working to de-escalate situations. When fighting is necessary, the Guard will normally seek to keep casualties to a minimum, restrict it in area and get it over quickly. In a battle for legitimacy, a state's armed forces operating on its own territory must seek to help, not harm.

As we will see when we look at the Air Force, the Air Guard will retain more conventional missions, missions that employ it overseas

as well as at home. However, its first priority also will become protecting and helping American citizens where they live.

If, as may happen, Fourth Generation war develops on American
soil to the point where our federal union is weakened or even begins
to come apart — a highly undesirable event probably brought on by
Washington acting illegitimately —, the Guard will take on another
function, one vital to preventing America's descent into what we now
see in places such as Syria and Libya. It must ensure that it is the *only*
militia in its state, and it must be prepared to use force if necessary to
establish and maintain its monopoly.

While the militia movement in America is weak at present, some
patriotic citizens have formed what they call "militias." In a time of
national disintegration, such militias would multiply. The National
Guard must act forcefully to compel such militias to operate under
the orders of the Guard at all times. Militias such as the "Cajun Navy"
along the Gulf of Mexico are helpful. Unarmed, equipped with the air
boats and other watercraft they use in civilian life, these militiamen
exist solely to rescue people in floods. The Guard should welcome
them, as they would welcome whatever support the Guard can give
them in performing their mission. They will know the local waterways
even better than the Guardsmen do (often, there will be personnel
overlap) and they can easily work together.

Armed militias, on the other hand, always present a risk. The
chaos that we see in Syria and Libya spawned multiple armed militias and they in turn make any restoration of the state and of order
impossible. If our federal union is disintegrating, similar militias will
form here. The Guard must give them a stark choice: disband or put
themselves completely under the Guard's orders. The first order they
receive from the Guard is likely to get rid of their weapons. If they
refuse, the Guard must be prepared to use force to disarm them (that
usually won't be necessary because many of the people in each group
will know each other). Wandering groups of armed men are the worst
plague that can afflict a place where the state has failed. We cannot let

them form here, and the National Guard, supported where necessary by the regular armed forces (if they still exist), must prevent them by any means necessary.

All this may sound rather radical. But these are the radical changes Fourth Generation war thrusts upon us. At the very least, we must begin to think about them and prepare. To paraphrase Trotsky, you may not be interested in Fourth Generation war, but Fourth Generation war is interested in you.

The Coast Guard

Like the National Guard, the Coast Guard usually comes last in books and papers about the U.S. armed services. Like the National Guard, Fourth Generation war changes that. The Coast Guard becomes our most important active-duty service, because it does what its name says: it guards our coasts.

As we will see when we look at the other active-duty forces, America reaps vast defensive advantages from the fact that geographically we are almost an island. Controlling who moves across our shorelines is a great deal easier than controlling passage through our land frontiers, as we know all too well from our southern border. At the same time, it is imperative that we effectively control access to and transit across our shorelines, because undesirable or even threatening people and things will seek to land — to an ever greater degree, in fact, as Fourth Generation war and its effects spread. The Coast Guard's mission is to stop them, and our security depends on it doing so.

The Coast Guard is also by far our least expensive active-duty service. Its annual budget is just over $12 billion. For that it gives us 56,569 coastguardsmen and 1,893 ships and boats, most of them small, as they should be for coastal waters. For that, not only do we get border security but also, as in the case of the National Guard, important help in peacetime to American civilians. In all our waters, the Coast

Guard keeps navigation safe and rescues people on the water who run into trouble. Those services alone would justify its small cost.

The Coast Guard is, in fact, at present under-resourced for its twin missions of maritime safety and border control. And maritime border control will be challenged more often and more forcefully as Fourth Generation war spreads, entities such as drug cartels grow, and immigrants from the Global South become more desperate to invade the Global North. While the Navy should be made available to back up the Coast Guard wherever necessary (and then be put under the Coast Guard's command), we will probably need to raise the Coast Guard's budget at the same time we cut spending on our other regular forces. In a world of Fourth Generation war, defending America gets a higher priority than playing games on the far side of the world.

The Navy

To see where the Navy needs to go, we need to look at three of its components. The first is our fleet of fourteen "boomers," the submarines that carry long-range ballistic missiles with nuclear warheads. As an important part of our nuclear deterrent, they should be retained and, when necessary, replaced. The Navy argues it is at that point now, but before we spend billions on new ballistic missile subs, we should see if a Service Life Extension Program is possible. That would postpone replacing the current "boomers" until the federal budget is less out of balance than at present.

Reconfiguring the U.S. Navy for Fourth Generation war is the second component, and it is not expensive. What it requires is that the Navy equip and train itself to take control of a region's coastal and inland waters. In much of the world, the only reasonably safe, afford-able, and sometimes possible way to move is by water. In the Congo, where a journey that under the Belgians took an hour now takes a day, the Congo river is the main highway. As states weaken and fail, land transport also fails. The trains cease to run as the Westerners or

Chinese who maintained the engines go home. The highways become infested with bandits and militias. As was true for the whole world until the coming of the railway in the 19th century, everything depends on water transport. Water unites and land divides.

In such situations, whoever controls use of the waterways — coastal, riverine, and lake — has a tremendous advantage. He decides who can move and who cannot. We need a U.S. Navy that gives us that ability anywhere in the world.

This is especially important for the United States because it allows us to shape local situations without having to invade and occupy a country, something we want to avoid doing with U.S. forces even when we are acting as part of the alliance of all states. In Fourth Generation war, power flows to anyone who can affect local balances of power, shifting them to or from one or another contender depending on who does our will. Those local balances of power are what most of the players care most about. They will be willing, even eager, to make deals with whatever outside force can affect them. If we control most transportation by controlling the waterways, that will be us. That will give us the leverage we need to help strengthen or restore the state, and to do so with little or no fighting. In Fourth Generation war, victory comes more often through de-escalation than through escalation.

At present, the U.S. Navy has little or no capability in coastal or inland waters. Why? Because it sneers at the mission. This attitude is, regrettably, part of the U.S. Navy's present-day culture. In the 1970s, when reformers in Congress attempted to give the Navy some small, fast missile boats suitable to coastal waters, the Chief of Naval Operations opposed them, testifying to the House Armed Services Committee, "The U.S. Navy has no place for little ships." This was as ignorant as it was ironic, because our navy has a long tradition of coastal, inland, and riverine operations, reaching from the South Vietnamese delta back to Union Navy operations on the Confederacy's rivers to our victories over the British on Lake Erie and Lake Champlain during the War of 1812.

So averse to coastal and riverine waters has today's U.S. Navy become that it even has a rule decreeing a ship commander must be relieved, ending his career, if his ship touches ground. In coastal and riverine waters, ships run aground all the time. U.S. Navy skippers are so terrified by this rule that, according to European navies who routinely train to fight in coastal waters, they become laughingstocks in exercises. One Scandinavian navy showed Mr. Lind a video of one of their own fast missile boats that, training at night, had run its hull completely up out of the water on a rock. Mr. Lind asked if the skipper was relieved. They laughed and said, "Of course not."

In recent years, the U.S. Navy has built some so-called "littoral combat ships" for coastal waters. Unfortunately, they typify current Navy shipbuilding. They are far too expensive to use in coastal waters where mines and shore-based missiles will be common, costing almost half a billion dollars apiece. They are "hi-tech," which means they are unreliable and cannot be repaired with what is available locally in Third World regions. And they stick out like sore thumbs as foreign warships, when you want to be as inconspicuous as possible.

Real "littoral (and riverine) combat ships" are modified commercial craft, most often fishing boats. They are stealthy because they have the same signatures as other fishing boats. They are cheap to build and operate, with modular weapons and sensors that are normally concealed. Their hulls and power plants can be repaired locally and they can run on local fuel. Their goal should be to blend in, not stand out: "Walk softly but carry a big stick" is good advice in Fourth Generation conflicts.

Again, building a riverine and coastal waters capability for Fourth Generation situations is not expensive. It will cost but a small fraction of what we will save by reshaping the Navy for a world where wars between states are unlikely and undesirable. That leads us in turn to the third component of our affordable, relevant U.S. Navy: our "insurance force."

The United States is by geography a maritime nation. Our oceans are our best security and our most defensible borders. Even as war between states exits history's stage, prudence, that highest of conservative virtues,[2] dictates that we remain a naval power. We need not be supreme in every sea. But we must maintain clear naval supremacy in the North Atlantic, the Pacific up to the waters around Australia and New Zealand, and the Caribbean. We should remain able to participate in conflicts in other seas and oceans as well, as part of coalitions. We should do this not because we anticipate, much less desire, naval confrontations with Russia, China, or any other state, but as insurance. We should always retain the unquestioned ability to control the waters around us, waters leading to our shores, because that is what our geography demands.

To that end, we need to maintain a navy still able to fight and defeat other state navies. As has usually been true in history, that in turn means we must remain the world's strongest navy in capital ships. Today's capital ship is the submarine.

World War II saw the aircraft carrier replace the battleship as the capital ship, the type of ship on which command of the oceans depends. But almost unnoticed, World War II saw the aircraft carrier itself relieved of that role. When, in April, 1945, the first German Type XXI U-boat went to sea, the crown as capital ship passed from the carrier to the submarine.

The Type XXI U-boat was the first true submarine. All submarines to that point had been submersible surface ships. They spent most of their time on the surface, because they had to. Their underwater top speed was low, only about 8 knots, and their batteries ran out of power in less than an hour at that speed. Most then had to surface to recharge their batteries. The Type XXI could run at 5 knots underwater for 75 hours, its top speed submerged was 17.5 knots and it used a snorkel to recharge so it never had to surface. The first Type XXI to go to sea

---

2   See *The Politics of Prudence* by Russell Kirk (ISI Press, Brun Mawr, PA. 1993).

literally played with an Allied anti-submarine hunter-killer group, deadly to other U-boats; the Allied ships were helpless against it. At that point, the submarine replaced the aircraft carrier as the capital ship. Today, in virtually every exercise involving both submarines and aircraft carriers, the subs sink the carriers. That is what defines a capital ship: no other ship type can survive against it.

The U.S. Navy today has about 50 attack submarines, all of them nuclear-powered. The Navy appears satisfied with that number. But as part of our retrenchment to a defense budget of $100 billion, not all the submarines we build in the future should be nuclear-powered. A modern conventional submarine, which can avoid even contacting the surface (i.e., snorkeling) for a week or more, performs better than a nuclear boat in some respects. It is quieter, which is important since most submarine detection is based on hearing a sub. It is smaller, which makes it handier in coastal waters and offers less of a signature to active sonars. It can dive just as deeply. And it costs far less to build and operate. An attack submarine of the *Virginia* class now being built for the U.S. Navy costs $2.8 billion, while a modern, high-performance conventional attack submarine can be bought for about $500 million.

Nuclear subs do have one advantage: an ability to deploy rapidly to any place in the world, thanks to their high cruising speed underwater, something a conventional boat cannot match. But in combat, submarines almost always move slowly to avoid making noise, so that advantage vanishes once the sub arrives on station.

Because our new National Defense Strategy does not foresee us in conflict with other states over control of waters half a world away, conventional submarines can meet our requirements at a lower cost, for part of the submarine force. They are just as capable as the far more expensive nuclear boats for protecting our own shores and home waters. In fact, they perform that mission better.

So far we have seen that we need to spend more on the Navy to develop forces suitable for coastal and riverine combat in Fourth Generation wars and we need to maintain our existing force of capital ships, i.e., submarines. So how do we save money on the Navy? The answer is, from our surface fleet.

The surface fleet includes aircraft carriers, cruisers and destroyers, whose prime function is protecting the carriers, and amphibious ships, ships that carry marines into combat. Most of the Navy's budget goes into building, maintaining, and operating these types of ships. And it is here where large savings are to be found.

Those savings do not arise primarily from building new types of surface ships, although, as we will see, we can and should do that. Rather, they come from operating the surface ships we have differently. That begins with redeploying them.

At present, the U.S. Navy keeps fleets, usually built around one or more aircraft carriers, in seas all around the globe. We have fleets in the Mediterranean, the Indian Ocean, the Pacific, and elsewhere. These "forward-deployed forces," as they are called, are enormously expensive. Why? Because of the "rotation base" they require. For each ship deployed forward, we need at least two similar ships in the fleet. One of these ships is receiving maintenance, one is working up its crew and only one, the ship forward deployed, is ready for combat. Often, the maintenance required by our very complex "hi-tech" warships is such that we need four or five ships in the fleet to provide a sufficient rotation base for one forward-deployed ship.

The first thing we would do, therefore, is end forward deployments. Ships' most important characteristic is that they are mobile. They can steam at 30 knots or more from U.S. ports — Norfolk, San Diego, Pearl Harbor — to where they are needed if a crisis erupts involving a hostile foreign country. Even before we form the alliance of all states our new National Defense Strategy seeks, we can safely make this change. Armies have to be forward deployed to be relevant. So do tactical aircraft. Ships do not.

Once we redeploy the U.S. Navy in home waters, the rotation base requirement is greatly reduced. At any given moment, we will still have some ships in maintenance and some crews in training. But ships that are based in home ports need far less maintenance than do ships that are constantly deployed. As we saw with the U.S. Navy hospital ship *Comfort* when New York City was overwhelmed by COVID-19, ships can if necessary be pulled out of some types of maintenance and made ready for action quickly. Ships with crews in training can train more intensively while the combat-ready ships deploy. By ending forward deployments, we can have most U.S. Navy warships combat-ready most of the time, which means the Navy needs far fewer ships.

Of course, as our intended alliance of all states — or initially the new Triple Alliance of the United States, China, and Russia — comes into being, we will need fewer warships designed to fight other state navies. Fourth Generation entities' navies will be made up of modified commercial vessels, almost all of them very small — fishing boats and the like —, similar to the ships we will deploy against them, in coastal and riverine waters. Our submarine fleet will give us all the insurance we need against the increasingly remote chance of a war with another state navy.

That is our first source of big savings on the Navy. The second comes to us from long ago, from the 18th and 19th centuries. What is it? Like the navies of those years, in times of peace, most U.S. Navy ships will be "in ordinary," or as we would say now, in reserve.

Through most of history, all navies kept most of their ships in reserve, with just skeleton crews for maintenance, in times of peace. Why? Because manning them in peacetime was too expensive. As it tends to, history has come full circle. Given America's debt and deficit levels, it is too expensive for us now.

Except for our submarines, in times of peace, most of the U.S. Navy's ships will, under our new strategy, be in reserve. They won't quite be "in mothballs," unmanned; they will have minimal crews, crews who do routine maintenance and can sail, though not fight, the ships without augmentation by reservists. They will be able to attain combat readiness fast enough, when their crews are brought up to wartime strength, in a world where we seek to avoid conflicts with other states. Should we be surprised, our capital ships will still be in commission and combat ready—more so than today because their forward deployments will also be reduced.

The key to rapid mobilization with reservists is a change in the Navy's manpower system. As in the classic European army reserve systems, a ship's crew will form all at once with new recruits (except for the small peacetime crew). Their terms of enlistment will all end at the same time, at which point they will go into reserve.

We will keep a few of every ship type in active service to train crews. We will have at least three reserve "classes," maybe more, reflecting how recently they served on active duty. On mobilization, they will go, together with their old shipmates, into a ship of the same type, where everyone will do the same job they did when on active duty. The "first class" reservists, who will have had the most recent experience, will be called up first, then other classes as needed. The higher their "class number," the more refresher training they will need. But long-time European army experience shows that crews can become proficient quickly so long as the reserve system keeps the same men working together in the same jobs. Our current "shake and bake" reserve system, which moves people around as individuals, fails to do this, which makes our Naval Reserve only marginally useful. The new reserve system outlined here will make the Naval Reserve the bulk and backbone of the surface ship Navy. Of course, reservists cost a great deal less than do active-duty sailors unless the reserve is mobilized.

This brings us, finally, to the ships themselves. Most of our surface warships—the cruisers and destroyers—are of marginal utility in war. They exist primarily to protect the aircraft carriers from submarines, missiles, and bombers, but they do that job poorly at high unit cost. Against submarines, they deploy one or two helicopters, which can be effective in hunting subs. But one or two for a ship that costs more than a billion dollars is hardly cost-effective (the carriers also carry anti-submarine helicopters of their own.)

To protect the carriers from enemy aircraft and missiles, our cruisers and destroyers rely on a radar and missile system called "Aegis," for Zeus's shield. Unfortunately, like Zeus's shield, it is mythical. It has never been tested realistically against low-flying, fast missiles, much less against anti-ship ballistic missiles in the terminal stages of their flights (and employing decoys). Its ability to shoot such missiles (and even low-flying aircraft) down is highly suspect. Nor can these "warships" take a hit themselves. With no armor and hulls packed full of electronics, they are likely to be knocked out of action by a single hit. We saw that in the "tanker war" in the Persian Gulf, where the tankers ended up escorting the "warships" because the tankers could take hits and the "warships" could not. We also saw it when a suicide boat almost sank the destroyer U.S.S. *Cole.*

As if that picture were not grim enough, should we make the absurd strategic blunder of getting into a war with China or Russia, Aegis is likely to prove ineffective because the incoming anti-ship missiles will probably have nuclear warheads. After the Cold War ended, the U.S. Navy received a shock when it found out the Soviets planned to go nuclear at sea from the outset. It doesn't take many missiles getting by Aegis (called "leakers") when each one has a nuclear warhead. The Navy's planned Charge of the Light Brigade with its carriers against the Kola Peninsula would have ended quickly. When Admiral Hyman Rickover, the father of the nuclear-propelled U.S. Navy, was asked in a Senate hearing how long he thought the carriers would last in a war with the Soviet Union, his reply was, "About two days."

Our eleven aircraft carriers and eight carrier-type amphibious ships (LHAs) will remain useful, because big ships with large hangers and flat decks can carry many things, not just aircraft. Unlike current practice, the carriers do not need to have standardized air wings aboard. They can carry any type of aircraft that can take off from them and land on them. They, and the large amphibious ships such as the LPDs and LSDs, can carry troops, set field hospitals up on board, be filled with materials for disaster relief—whatever is appropriate to the situation. With our expanded definition of national defense and more frequent violent weather, these ships' roles in disaster relief could become more important than their functions as aircraft carriers or amphibious assault ships.

However, along with the cruisers and destroyers, they should be the last of their kind. There is another way to get the capabilities they provide, one that is cheaper both to buy and to operate and that can give us real warships, ships that can take hits and keep on fighting.

How is this possible? If flows from two major changes in ship design.

For the first time since the 17th century, merchant ship hulls and propulsion plants can offer the same levels of protection and speed as do those of purpose-built warships. In recent decades, the world has seen some merchant ships that can steam at sustained speeds of more than thirty knots. Merchant ships can be designed to be more survivable, not less, than so-called warships, because merchant tonnage is cheap. That means the ships can be built much larger than is necessary to carry their intended sensors and weapons, and the space can be filled with something fireproof that floats. Most anti-ship missiles have shaped-charge warheads, and our new-model warships can defeat those with "water armor:" water-filled cells lining the sides of the ships where battleships carried their heaviest armor. Other than the aircraft carriers, our navy's ships have no armor, and their sensors and weapons are packed in small spaces so one hit disables them. The new merchant-ship-based warships we propose would be far more survivable.

The second development in ship design, or more precisely in the design of weapons and sensors, is that they can be modularized. Our new-model warships would have standardized receptacles where whatever weapons and sensors the mission required could simply be plugged in. The German shipyard Blohm & Voss did this decades ago with their MEKO-class frigates. As a test, they reconfigured one ship from an anti-aircraft mission to an anti-submarine mission in one weekend.

All future warships, including aircraft carriers, would have merchant-ship hulls and propulsion. The carriers would be flat-decked merchantmen, i.e. containerships, with containerized aircraft support facilities.

Not only would they be less expensive to buy, they would be much cheaper to operate, especially in peacetime. In time of peace, our new-model warships would mostly be in (subsidized) merchant service. That would go a long way to rebuild our sadly neglected merchant marine. Their crews would be naval reservists, who on mobilization would just keep doing their peacetime jobs of running the ship. The sailors to man the weapons and sensors would be mobilized reservists who had crewed on a similar ship during the time they were on active duty. They too would be doing their old jobs, with their old shipmates. Regardless of where in the country they came from, they could train locally because weapon and sensor modules could be put anywhere for refresher training purposes. Like the reservists themselves, they would be collected on mobilization and married up with the ships.

From the U.S. Navy's perspective, the problem is that these ships do not fit their mental picture of a warship. They will look like typical old merchant tubs, not "greyhounds of the sea." Our view is, if the seeming merchant ships are more survivable than the greyhounds, just as well armed and a whole lot cheaper, well, sailor, get used to it. Popeye won fights, not beauty contests.

Where this all leaves us is with a navy fully capable of defending us against hypothetical (and unlikely) threats from other states — more capable than the navy we have now in the coastal and inland waters where Fourth Generation enemies will be encountered — and a great deal more affordable. We are actually being more generous to the Navy than to the other services, because America's geography makes us a maritime country. The really big savings are yet to come.

The Army

They start with the U.S. Army. The same geography that requires that we have a strong navy also means the United States does not need an army. For most of our country's history, we did not really have one, and that worked just fine.

The driving strategic fact is that, then and now, we face no threat across our land frontiers with Canada or Mexico, at least in the form of other state armies with tanks, artillery, hockey pucks (Canada), etc. We do face a serious Fourth Generation threat from Mexico, in the forms of immigration and trans-border activities by drug cartels. As already noted, we need extensive passive defenses along our southern frontier to deal with these threats. But that border should be manned by the Border Patrol, backed up by the National Guard. It does not need active-duty forces; indeed, unless they were rotated frequently as the Guard units will be, they would soon be suborned by the traffickers.

In our country's history, we have built large armies only when war required them. Wisely, we went back to a small army when those wars ended, with the exception of World War II. Then, the Cold War seemed to require we maintain a large army in peacetime. Whether that was the real case or not, the Cold War is over, except for a small holdout in Korea, where South Korea is quite capable of defending itself conventionally.

With our new National Defense Strategy pointing our armed forces away from wars with other states and toward Fourth Generation wars, which we will fight as part of the Triple Alliance, we can again return to our historic small army. Even if someone were to postulate the strategic absurdity of wars with China or Russia, does anyone think we would fight big land wars on the Eurasian continent? To put such wars in perspective, in World War II, the German Army that attacked Russia in June, 1941, had more than three million men. The few armored or mechanized brigades the current U.S. Army could offer for such a war would be a tin whistle in a hurricane. Nor do we now have the industrial base to build more than 87,000 aircraft in one year, as we did in World War II. In terms of a conflict on the Eurasian land mass, today's U.S. Army is just a club of World War II reenactors (they even have the uniforms!).

What sort of army do we need for our new National Defense Strategy? We want to keep most of our Special Operations forces, including Special Forces itself (the Green Berets), Delta and the Ranger Regiment. Beyond these forces, which are useful in Fourth Generation war, the active duty Army should be reduced to three brigades: one armor, one light infantry, and one air defense. These should all be what the Germans call "Lehr" units, meaning they should focus on developing new tactics, testing new equipment, and instructing other similar units should we ever need to raise any. The light infantry brigade, which should be true light infantry (*Jägers*), not just line infantry with less equipment, would have a significant training role with the National Guard, while the armor and air defense brigades would be available to train similar foreign forces should we need to do that. In crises overseas, local allies sometimes want the U.S. to augment their air defense capabilities, a job that would fall to the air defense brigade.

Again, we cannot put exact numbers on this force — we happily leave that to the budgeteers — but we are looking at a U.S. Army of fewer than 40,000 men on active duty. Other than the Special Operations forces, their main real-world mission will be supporting the National Guard when the Guard needs them, which will be seldom.

The Air Force

The United States Air Force was founded on a lie. The lie was, and is, "winning through air power," the notion that bombardment from the sky can win wars all by itself. It has yet to do so.

Air power has been important in war when it has been integrated with the operations of land and sea forces. That, unfortunately, is anathema to the Air Force. Since its founding, it has striven tirelessly to disconnect itself from both the Army and the Navy. Because war requires the opposite, in our reformed, $100-billion military, the Air Force largely disappears.

If that comes as a shock, remember that we are no longer planning to fight other states with air forces of their own. We will retain a residual capability to do that as insurance, much as with the Navy. But neither that residuum, nor the (limited) air power that is useful in Fourth Generation war, requires we have an active-duty Air Force beyond those elements that are part of our strategic nuclear deterrent, i.e., the guys who sit in holes with their missiles. (We do not plan to continue the charade of fighting nuclear wars with other major powers by sending in "penetrating bombers.")

The reasons we do not need an active-duty Air Force are two. First, air power has only limited utility in Fourth Generation war. It is useful for reconnaissance and airborne logistics. There is no role for fighter aircraft, because the enemy has no airplanes. That could change as Fourth Generation entities make greater use of drones. Ironically, the sort of fighters that would be effective against drones are not hyper-expensive F-22s but cheap, simple, World War II or even World War I fighters. The Red Baron's Fokker Dr-1 triplane would be perfect for shooting down drones, with its low speed but high maneuverability. It would be cheap to build, and we suspect we would have fighter pilots willing to pay to fly it.

But for the most part, attack aviation, whether manned aircraft or drones, is not only useless but counterproductive in Fourth Generation war. The evidence is in, and it is clear. In our twenty years of war in Afghanistan, and almost as many in Somalia and Iraq, we have launched endless airstrikes. Yet we have lost all those wars. The two are connected. When we hit mud-walled Afghan compounds in the middle of the night, killing men, women, and children, we recruit new enemies faster than our airstrikes can kill old ones. The enemy, enraged at being hit by enemies who run no risk, become hydras, growing multiple new heads for every one we airstrike off. We win on the physical and tactical levels of war at the expense of losing on the strategic and moral levels. In war, a higher level trumps a lower. So we lose the wars. No "hi-tech" or "precision strike" is likely to change this.

There is one big exception, which we touched on previously. After a big hit on American soil by a foreign Fourth Generation war entity, such as that on 9/11, we need to strike back immediately and massively. The target would be both the entity that attacked us and the place where it is based. Our purpose in this retaliation would be annihilation, both of the attacker and its host. It should be intentionally disproportionate.[3] Assuming the attacker is based in a weak, failing or failed state, we will face little air opposition and no danger of state retaliation. In such a situation, we may both need and desire to employ nuclear weapons. However, it will generally be better if we do not have to. Here, what we require is the ability to launch massive airstrikes that will, in a matter of days if not hours, kill as many people and destroy as much property as would a nuclear weapon. This is doable. It requires manned bombers, but not sophisticated ones. We need a force of simple "bomb trucks," a role now filled by our B-52s, that can lay down vast tonnage of explosives quickly.

At some point, the remaining B-52s will have to be replaced, but their replacements should not be expensive. They should not be the very costly manned "penetrating bomber" the Air Force is now seeking. A modified civilian air freighter should be able to do the job.

The second reason we do not need an active-duty Air Force is that we have multiple other air forces. Both the Navy and the Marine Corps have air forces of their own. And, we have two other air forces that perform better and cost less than the active-duty Air Force: the

---

3   Martin Van Creveld calls this the "Hama Model" after Syrian President Hafez
     al-Assad's destruction of the city of Hama by a massive artillery bombardment
     when that city rebelled.

Air Reserve and the Air National Guard, which we would amalgamate under the Guard.

In exercise after exercise, the Guard and the Reserve outperform the regular Air Force. Why? One important reason is personnel stability. In the Reserve and the Guard, the same people fly and maintain the same aircraft for many years. In all our active-duty forces, people are constantly moved around. Our reforms would reduce that, but the personnel churn is still likely to be higher than in the Reserve and Guard.

Beyond the boys in their holes with their ICBMs, we would move all remaining Air Force missions into the amalgamated Reserve and Guard. That would include the legacy fighter and fighter-bomber capabilities we would retain as insurance (especially the A-10) and the small number of recon and transport aircraft we would need for Fourth Generation war. Our expanded definition of national defense would lead us to retain a robust air transport capability to help Americans caught up in natural disasters. Additional air transport capability is always available from civilian airlines.

The Air National Guard would do its own pilot training. When it needs new aircraft, it would hold competitions with whatever aircraft the world market offers. These competitions would be real fly-offs and shoot-offs, not "computer simulations" that reflect the old GIGO principle (Garbage In, Garbage Out). If a foreign design wins, we would build it here under license.

Not surprisingly, an Air Force founded on a lie has come to the inevitable end of everything so founded. Repeated failures left the fraud obvious for all to see. The Navy's and Marine Corps' aircraft are already integrated with our sea and land forces. We should salute the Air Force and the men who served in it as it passes into history, an idea that failed, as so many ideas have failed in war. Our $100-billion defense budget cannot afford to pay for a myth, the myth of "winning through air power." No one has, and no one will.

The Marine Corps

The United States Marine Corps should become our force of choice for Fourth Generation war overseas, and it should be restructured, re-equipped and retrained for this mission.

Why? There are two reasons. The first is that projection of anything beyond a token ground force to other seas and continents requires that force to be sea-mobile and sea-based. This is difficult to improvise. We will be better served by a land force that is married permanently to the sea, and the Marine Corps is. It is part and parcel of the Navy, and as such offers the most useful land force for a country that is by geography a sea power.

Note that what is important here is the Marine Corps' seaborne mobility, not its ability to undertake opposed amphibious landings. The latter have remained the Marine Corps' boast since World War II, but they are largely irrelevant to Fourth Generation war. Few if any Fourth Generation war entities will be able to mount more than a trivial beach defense, and they are not likely to attempt even that. If opposed amphibious landings are no longer the Marine Corps' focus, it will not need equipment specialized for that mission, which is usually expensive.

The other reason the Marine Corps, not the Army, should be our land force of choice for Fourth Generation war is that of all our armed services, the Marine Corps has advanced furthest toward becoming a Third Generation force. While that is not sufficient to win Fourth Generation wars, it is a necessary precondition. A Second Generation military that reduces war to putting firepower on targets is certain to lose Fourth Generation wars.[4] Despite occasional attempts to move beyond it, the U.S. Army is still stuck fast in the Second Generation.

In contrast, in the early 1990s the Marine Corps adopted Third Generation maneuver warfare as its official doctrine. It wrote some excellent field manuals and began the free-play training that

---

4   Unless the Hama Model is being employed.

maneuver warfare requires. Regrettably, its progress toward the Third Generation stopped at that point. The required fundamental changes in its personnel system, education and training were not made, with the result that the Marine Corps today can talk about maneuver warfare but cannot do it. That leaves it ahead of the Army, but with a long way to go.

Fortunately, the current Marine Corps Commandant, General David Berger, indicated when he took office that he intends to make the changes in personnel, education and training maneuver warfare demands. It is too early to determine how successful he will be; resistance by various internal bureaucracies will be stubborn. Regrettably, he has shown no interest in what the country needs most, a force competent at Fourth Generation war. That is a matter where the initiative will have to come from the White House and the Secretary of Defense. When it does, the Marine Corps will still be ahead of our other services in terms of its ability to respond.

These considerations lead us to propose a Marine Corps that would be similar in structure to that we have at present, which is to say it would have its own aviation and be organized, as public law requires, into three divisions and three air wings. Much would change inside that structural framework, including that, as has occurred world-wide, the divisions would become smaller. We envision a total manpower strength of the Marine Corps at around 50,000 men, which would make it the largest of our active-duty services.

It is important to keep in mind that in most Fourth Generation conflicts, we will be a part of an international coalition, based on the Triple Alliance and including all states. Our main role will seldom be fighting; as has recently been the case in Somalia, most if not all ground forces will be from other regional states that are better attuned to the local culture and less casualty-sensitive.

But as with the Air Force, which is to say the amalgamated Air Reserve and Air National Guard, we will occasionally have to be the lead or even sole force when we are responding to a devastating attack on the American homeland. The Air Force's role would be in bombing for annihilation. The Marine Corps' role would be raids.

These raids would also have annihilation as their goal. As we said earlier, our response to successful major attacks on American soil should be Roman. In raids, the Marines' mission would be to de-populate the region that served as the attackers' base and physically destroy its entire infrastructure, leaving "no stone on stone." When our Marines depart, the area they raided should be like Carthage at the end of the Third Punic War; they should sow the soil with salt as they withdraw.

Why would we choose raids instead of air attacks? Air attacks may do the job in cities, but not in the countryside. Those who attacked us may be based in the latter. Also, actions on the ground always have a more powerful mental and moral impact than do air attacks. We will have shown our enemy that we can fight him man-to-man and eyeball-to-eyeball. We will have met him on his own soil and won. Others contemplating similar attacks on our country will not think Americans are weak, cowardly, or lacking in will.

Obviously, the size of our raiding force will depend on the situa-tion. But we have difficulty imagining a situation where a 50,000-man Marine Corps would not be adequate to do the job. Again, in most cases we will not be fighting alone. Even if we wanted to go it alone in response to another 9/11, as a matter of national anger and pride, 50,000 Marines should be enough. If they aren't, we will also have a Marine Corps Reserve.

Summary

Again, we cannot put a precise dollar total on the forces we have proposed. Because active-duty sailors, soldiers, airmen and marines would be few and manpower is our military's greatest expense, we expect the forces outlined here will move us a long way toward an affordable defense budget.

But the savings don't end yet. The last thing we need to reform, where reform can save many hundreds of billions of dollars, is our system for developing and purchasing military equipment. As we noted earlier, at present that system looks distressingly like the old Soviet economy. By moving toward a free market approach to R&D and procurement, we are certain that we can get better equipment at much lower costs.

Acquisition

THE PROCESS by which we develop and acquire military equipment reflects the intellectually stagnant, bureaucratic culture of the military it serves. No matter how simple (ATVs) or complex (fighter jets) the end product is, all programs must follow a rigid acquisition process with endless milestones, phases and rules. Yet despite this complexity, the system has no checks and balances to determine if the hardware serves the National Defense Strategy, meets a real military need, or works under combat conditions. The result is weapon systems that cost, in the case of the F-35 fighter/bomber, more than a trillion dollars over their life cycles—for an aircraft that will probably never be used to do more than drop bombs on peasants. It is the same for other systems across the board.

It gets worse. The armed services have developed a system of "strategic contracting" that guarantees even the biggest turkeys never get cancelled. "Strategic contracting" means placing so many subcontracts in so many states and congressional districts that senators and congressmen defend the program in order to protect constituents' jobs. The disastrous F-35 (America's H-177) is built in 45 of our 50 states.

One might think that when the members of our armed services who actually fight perceive a need, we would first try to meet it by adapting existing equipment, changing our tactics or techniques, or buying something adequate to the job that is available on the open market. None of that happens. Instead, a vast, new, multi-billion dollar program is created that "pushes the envelope" with the most expensive new technology and takes almost a decade to produce a product—which is often then already obsolete. The Marine Corps recently said it needs a new armored fighting vehicle to replace the current Light Armored Vehicle because ISIS is dropping anti-vehicle bomblets from drones. That program will cost billions and take years, when all they need to do is put a chicken-wire awning over the existing vehicle to set off the bomblets' fuzes prematurely.

This endless, convoluted process is run by an army of civilian bureaucrats, thousands of personnel per weapon system. They all know that any measures to simplify or speed up the process threaten their jobs. Those jobs mostly consist of navigating reams of Federal Acquisition Regulations and producing thousands of legally required documents that no one reads. In all this vast, Soviet-style bureaucracy, the business of selecting and delivering hardware is almost an afterthought.

When you need a new car, you buy "off the shelf." You visit various car company showrooms, see what is available and buy what most closely meets your need. The current acquisition process makes almost no use of "off-the-shelf" buys. Instead, every requirement leads to a new development contract for something that does not now exist. How much do you think a car would cost if you went to, say, your local Ford showroom, gave them a highly detailed list of characteristics you want your new car to have, then told them to design and build one just for you?

While the Defense Department will tell you it uses "competition" to get better products at lower prices, its definition of "competition" is not what you might think. It is restricted to the same old contractors, over and over. The complexity of the acquisition process makes it almost impossible for new companies to enter. Even among the usual suspects, contracts are usually split up so everybody gets something. Seldom is there a "shoot-off" or "fly-off" among competing designs; such tests are "simulations" done in labs, where the old rule of "Garbage In, Garbage Out" applies. And even after these lame "competitions," the results are often ignored to favor preferred contractors.

To top it all off, the whole process ignores such questions as whether the system can be maintained by military personnel under combat conditions and if it can be produced affordably in adequate numbers. The "stealth" F-22 fighter is so complex that it needs maintenance for every 20 minutes of flight time. And which do you think would help you most to win a war, 19 "Stealth" B-2 bombers or, for about the same price, 30,000 Stukas?

How do we clean this Augean stable? We replace our Gosplan, the old Soviet central planning agency, with a free market.

To do that, we need to take three broad actions:

- "Flatten the organization" by eliminating almost all of the current acquisition bureaucracy;

- change from a process-based system to one that is results-focused; and

- apply the idea of subsidiarity to acquisition, which means needs and problems are dealt with at the lowest-possible level. The system is bottom-up rather than top-down.

Here is how it should work. A need or problem is identified by the users — the front-line soldiers, sailors, airmen or marines who actually fight. They first seek not a new piece of hardware but a tactical or technical solution, which they do through an open-architecture system where everyone can offer an idea.

If that does not meet the need, they look for ways to adapt existing equipment to do so. That equipment may have been designed for a different purpose or may come from a different armed service. In World War II, the German Army's deadly 88 mm. anti-tank gun was designed as an anti-aircraft gun for the Luftwaffe.

If none of these approaches work, the service in question looks to see what new equipment is available on the world-wide open market. If possible, they buy something designed to compete for civilian buyers in the free market. Why? Because such equipment usually costs less and is much more robust. If the users find they prefer a foreign system and the buy is a large one, we build it here in America under license.

Only if all this fails to meet the users' need do we design and build an all-new piece of military hardware. That process begins with a broad statement of what the new equipment must *do*, not what it must *be*. Then, the process is opened to design competition, again on a world-wide basis. The winner is chosen based on real shoot-offs and fly-offs, with the intended users doing the flying, shooting, and maintaining. When we did this in the 1980s to obtain a new fighter and a new ground-attack aircraft, we got the superb F-16 and A-10, aircraft that performed better than their predecessors and cost less. Needless to say, the current acquisition system made sure that never happened again.

To keep this system both honest and efficient, instead of relying on thousands of pages of rules and regulations, it should be overseen by a small number, probably about twenty, of "Financial Generals." The French armed forces currently have such generals. They often go straight from Army or Air Force captain rank to four-star general. For the remainder of their careers, they will have no other job but to make sure the government and the taxpayer get their money's worth. They have broad authority, sufficient so they can look into anything and order anything to that end. In our new system, they would be forbidden to work directly or indirectly for any company doing business with the government after their retirement, on pain of a prison sentence.

The approach we have described here would meet the three goals of flattening the organization, changing from a process-based to a results-based acquisition system, and making that system work bottom-up instead of top-down. It would also greatly reduce our research & development costs and the cost of new systems while giving our men on the front-line better gear faster. The only losers would be the thousands of federal bureaucrats who would forfeit their high-paying jobs, our state capitalist large defense companies, and the old Soviet economy, which would lose its last remaining outpost.

Conclusion

THIS SHORT BOOK describes two large changes from our current defense posture. One of those should happen, and one will happen. The change that will happen is a massive reduction in our defense spending. It will be driven not by choice but by necessity. The rate at which governments around the world, including our own, are printing money and piling up debt will bring a world-wide debt crisis and depression. Only the timing is uncertain; the event is inevitable. When that happens, the U.S. and most other nations will no longer be able to borrow money at rates they can afford. Drastic cuts in spending, including for defense, will come because there will be no alternative. As we said at the outset, our country may not be able to afford a defense budget as high as $100 billion.

The change which should come is restructuring our armed services for a world where the primary threat will be the collapse of states and of the state system itself. The threat that presents, of anarchy and Old Night swallowing the world, far outweighs any dangers we may face from other states. Our armed services, which are powerful against other states that fight as we do (less so against any that don't), are unsuited to meet this threat, the threat posed by Fourth Generation war. Like most other state armed forces, whenever they have fought non-state, Fourth Generation enemies, they have lost.

If the Washington establishment is in charge of the defense budget cuts the coming debt crisis will mandate, we will end up with smaller versions of the armed forces we have now. They will, in effect, be toys, to be trotted out for parades and other public displays. Given how few "trigger pullers" we field now, with defense spending at about a trillion dollars a year, we will then have virtually no combat capability at all

We have no illusions; the changes called for in this book to the shape of our armed services, changes intended to reorient them from fighting states to upholding states, will only come if anti-establishment forces take over in Washington. The election of Donald Trump as president shows that can happen. His subsequent defeat tells us how powerful the Washington establishment remains. Which will triumph in the end we do not know. But to those outside the establishment who are working for reform, military and civilian, we have here offered a road map to relevant armed forces at an affordable price.

OTHER BOOKS PUBLISHED BY ARKTOS

OTHER BOOKS PUBLISHED BY ARKTOS

OTHER BOOKS PUBLISHED BY ARKTOS

OTHER BOOKS PUBLISHED BY ARKTOS

SRI SRI RAVI SHANKAR

Celebrating Silence
Know Your Child
Management Mantras
Patanjali Yoga Sutras
Secrets of Relationships

GEORGE T. SHAW (ED.)

A Fair Hearing

FENEK SOLÈRE

Kraal

OSWALD SPENGLER

The Decline of the West
Man and Technics

RICHARD STOREY

The Uniqueness of Western Law

TOMISLAV SUNIC

Against Democracy and Equality
Homo Americanus
Postmortem Report
Titans are in Town

ASKR SVARTE

Gods in the Abyss

HANS-JÜRGEN SYBERBERG

On the Fortunes and Misfortunes
of Art in Post-War Germany

ABIR TAHA

Defining Terrorism
The Epic of Arya (2nd ed.)
Nietzsche's Coming God, or the
Redemption of the Divine
Verses of Light

JEAN THIRIART

Europe: An Empire of 400 Million

BAL GANGADHAR TILAK

The Arctic Home in the Vedas

DOMINIQUE VENNER

For a Positive Critique
The Shock of History

HANS VOGEL

How Europe Became American

MARKUS WILLINGER

A Europe of Nations
Generation Identity

ALEXANDER WOLFHEZE

Alba Rosa
Rupes Nigra

www.ingramcontent.com/pod-product-compliance
Lightning Source LLC
Chambersburg PA
CBHW032119280326
41933CB00009B/910